THE INDIAN FOLK ARTS AND CRAFTS

AN EXPLORATION OF INDIA'S REGIONAL FOLK ARTS AND CRAFTS

DR. JAGADEESH PILLAI

|| "Dedicated to all who seek to understand and appreciate Indian culture and tradition." ||

Contents

Contents

Prayer

"Om Asato Maa Sadgamaya, Tamaso Maa Jyotir Gamaya, Mrityor Maa Amritam Gamaya, Om Shantih, Shantih, Shantih"

The true meaning of this mantra is: OM guide me from the unreal to the real, from darkness to light, and from mortality to immortality.
OM Peace, Peace, Peace.

ABOUT THE AUTHOR

Dr. Jagadeesh Pillai is a renowned Guinness World Record holder, writer, and researcher hailing from Varanasi, also known as the abode of Lord Shiva. With a Ph.D. in Vedic Science and a range of creative ideas and achievements, he is a true polymath. He is the author of more than 100 books including Research Publications. Although his roots can be traced back to Kerala, the people of Varanasi hold him in high regard and affectionately consider him one of their own.

Dr. Pillai has achieved four Guinness World Records in the following subjects:

"Script to Screen" - In this record, Dr. Pillai produced and directed an animation film within the shortest time possible, breaking the previous record set by Canadians. He has also received numerous national and international awards and recognitions for this achievement.

Longest Line of Postcards - For this record, Dr. Pillai created a line of 16,300 postcards on the occasion of the 163rd anniversary of Indian Postal Day. The event also included a questionnaire about the Indian flag.

Largest Poster Awareness Campaign - Dr. Pillai designed an awareness campaign on the subject of "Beti Bachao - Beti Padhao" (Save the Girl Child - Educate the Girl Child) to achieve this record.

Largest Envelope - In tribute to the Indian Prime Minister's

"Make in India" initiative, Dr. Pillai created a 4000 square meter envelope using waste paper to achieve this record.

Attempted - **70000 Candles on a 210 kg Cake** - To celebrate the 70th Indian Independence Day, Dr. Pillai attempted to light 70,000 candles on a 210 kg cake, which was recorded in World Records India.

Attempted - **Documentary on Dhamek Stupa of Sarnath in 17 Languages** - Dr. Pillai attempted to create a documentary on the Dhamek Stupa of Sarnath, dubbing it in 17 different languages. The result of this attempt is currently awaiting confirmation from the Guinness World Records.

Dr. Pillai is skilled in teaching the Bhagavad Gita, a Hindu scripture, and is popular among young people. He has helped many young people improve their lives through his motivational teachings.

In addition to teaching, he has composed and sung numerous Sanskrit Bhajans and patriotic songs.

He has also written and directed several short films and documentaries for awareness campaigns, and has volunteered with the police in both UP and Kerala to spread awareness about various issues through videos and photography.

Incredibly, he has produced and directed over 100 documentaries about the city of Varanasi, all on his own.

He has also helped and guided more than 25 boys and girls to achieve world records through creative and innovative methods. He is a multifaceted person who uses his intellect and the blessings given to him by God to excel in various areas. He is both a teacher and a student, always learning and teaching, and is able to master any subject he comes across.

He is a selfless social activist and motivational speaker who has overcome struggles and failures to become a successful and enthusiastic individual with a rich life experience.

In addition to his work with the Bhagavad Gita, he is also an efficient Tarot card reader, Astro-Vastu consultant, and a talented singer and composer. He has sung the entire Ram Charita Manas and Bhagavad Gita in his own compositions, and has sung the phrase "Lokah Samastha Sukhino Bhavantu" in 50 different languages. He is currently working on a detailed and scientific study of Vedas, Upanishads, Puranas, and the Bhagavad Gita. He has also composed and sung the Hanuman Chalisa and Gayatri Mantra in 108 and 1008 different compositions, respectively.

Awards - Four Times Guinness World Records, Winner of Mahatma Gandhi Vishwa Shanti Puraskar, Mahatma Gandhi Global Peace Ambassador, Kashi Ratna Award, Dr. APJ Abdul Kalam Motivational Person of the Year 2017, Mother Teresa Award, Indira Gandhi Priyadarshini Award, Bharat Vikas Ratna Award, Udyog Ratna Award, Vigyan Prasar Award, Poorvanchal Ratn Samman.

Preface

The Indian Folk Arts and Crafts: An Exploration of India's Regional Folk Arts and Crafts is a comprehensive guide to the traditional art forms that have been passed down through generations in India. The book delves into the various folk arts and crafts of different regions in India, highlighting their unique characteristics and the stories behind them.

The book begins with an introduction that explores the significance of Indian folk arts and crafts in the Indian cultural heritage. It also examines the impact of modernization on these traditional art forms and the efforts being made to preserve and promote them.

The book is divided into chapters that focus on the different regions of India. Each chapter explores the traditional folk arts and crafts of that region, including their history, techniques, and symbolism. The reader will discover the rich diversity of India's folk arts and crafts, from the Phad paintings of North India to the Tanjore paintings of South India, from the Warli paintings of West India to the Madhubani paintings of East India, and from the bamboo and cane crafts of Northeastern India to the traditional folk music, dance and festivals of India.

The book also includes beautiful photographs that showcase the intricate designs and vibrant colors of these traditional art forms. It is an essential resource for anyone interested in the cultural heritage of India and the traditional art forms that continue to be an important part of the country's identity.

This book is written for both general readers and specialists, it is a treasure trove of information on India's rich cultural heritage, providing an in-depth understanding of the country's folk arts and crafts and their significance in preserving the traditional way of life, customs, and beliefs of the Indian people. It is a must-read for anyone interested in Indian culture, art and heritage.

I

Introduction: The significance of Indian folk arts and crafts in the Indian cultural heritage

The Indian folk arts and crafts are an integral part of the Indian cultural heritage.

They are a reflection of the traditional way of life, customs, and beliefs of the people of India. Folk arts and crafts are a medium through which the traditional knowledge, skills, and creativity of the Indian people are passed down from generation to generation. These arts and crafts are not only a source of livelihood for many people in rural India but also a symbol of the rich cultural diversity that India possesses.

The Indian folk arts and crafts are diverse and varied, reflecting the different regions, cultures, and traditions of the country. From the intricate Phad paintings of Rajasthan to the colorful Madhubani paintings of Bihar, from the delicate Kutch embroidery of Gujarat to the intricate Tanjore paintings of Tamil Nadu, the Indian folk arts and crafts are a true reflection of the rich cultural heritage of India.

The Indian folk arts and crafts are not only a source of artistic expression but also a medium through which the traditional knowledge, skills, and creativity of the Indian people are passed down from generation to generation. These arts and crafts are a vital part of the Indian cultural heritage and help to preserve the traditional way of life and customs of the Indian people. They are also an important source of income for many people in rural India and help to promote the national identity of the country.

The Indian folk arts and crafts are also an important aspect of the Indian tourism industry. They attract many tourists from all over the world who come to India to explore the country's rich cultural heritage. The Indian folk arts and crafts are also an important source of revenue for the government and help to promote the national economy.

Indian folk arts and crafts are an integral part of the Indian cultural heritage. They are a reflection of the traditional way of life, customs, and beliefs of the people of India. They are a medium through which the traditional knowledge, skills, and creativity of the Indian people are passed down from generation to generation. They are an important source of livelihood for many people in rural India, a symbol of the rich cultural diversity of the country, and an important aspect of the Indian tourism industry.

"Indian folk art is the sweetest expression of the rural artisan", said the renowned art historian Mr. R.S. Shekhar. Indian folk art originated from the villages of India which unarguably have its own beauty, culture, and customs. It is considered as one of the oldest forms of art and continues to be cherished by the people of India. Indian folk art includes various kinds of art such as terracotta figures, puppet carving, wall paintings, block printing, jewelry making etc.

II

The Folk Arts of the North: An exploration of the traditional folk arts of North India

The Folk Arts of the North: An exploration of the traditional folk arts of North India, including Phad paintings, block printing, and blue pottery.

The folk arts of North India are a reflection of the rich cultural heritage of the region. They are an expression of the traditional way of life, customs, and beliefs of the people of North India. One of the most popular folk arts of North India is Phad painting. Phad paintings are large scrolls that depict the stories of the local deities and heroes. They are usually made on a piece of cloth or paper and are known for their vibrant colors and intricate details. Phad paintings are usually accompanied by a narrator who sings the story while the painting is unfurled.

Another traditional folk art of North India is block printing. Block printing is a technique of printing text or designs onto fabric or paper using wooden or metal blocks. The blocks are carved with the desired design and then dipped in ink. The ink is then pressed onto the fabric or paper to create the final print. Block printing is a popular folk art in Rajasthan and is known for its intricate designs and bright colors.

Blue pottery is also a traditional folk art of North India, particularly in Rajasthan. Blue pottery is a type of pottery that is made using a special type of glaze that gives the pottery a blue color. The pottery is made using a mixture of crushed quartz, borax, soda, and copper oxide. The pottery is then fired at a low temperature to give it its distinctive blue color. Blue pottery is known for its delicate and intricate designs.

The folk arts of North India are an important part of the cultural heritage of the region and are known for their vibrant colors, intricate designs, and traditional themes. These folk arts are an expression of the traditional way of life, customs, and beliefs of the people of North India. They are also an important source of income for many people in the region and help to promote the national identity of India.

ॐ

Designer Buddha Bot states "craft of India has in its heart the heart of ages". Crafts in India are extremely diverse, encompassing many communities and states; each carries its own unique identity and charm. Crafts are often seen as the lifelines of communities, providing economic and social support. They are linked to community beliefs, superstitions and rituals and are integral to a culture.

৪৩

III

The Folk Arts of the West: An exploration of the traditional folk arts of West India

The Folk Arts of the West: An exploration of the traditional folk arts of West India, including Warli paintings, Dholpur stone carvings, and Kutch embroidery.

The folk arts of West India are a reflection of the rich cultural heritage of the region. They are an expression of the traditional way of life, customs, and beliefs of the people of West India. One of the most popular folk arts of West India is Warli painting. Warli paintings are traditional tribal paintings that originated in the Warli tribe of

Maharashtra. They are known for their simplistic and geometric designs, which depict scenes from everyday life such as farming, hunting, and dance. The paintings are typically done on the walls of houses or on handmade paper or cloth using a mixture of rice paste, water and natural dyes.

Another traditional folk art of West India is Dholpur stone carvings. Dholpur is a small town in Rajasthan known for its intricate stone carvings. The stone carvings are made from a type of soft, fine-grained sandstone found in the region. The carvings typically depict Hindu gods and goddesses, as well as scenes from Hindu mythology. The carvings are known for their intricate details and fine craftsmanship.

Kutch embroidery is another traditional folk art of West India, particularly in Gujarat. Kutch embroidery is a type of hand-embroidery that is known for its intricate designs and vibrant colors. The embroidery is typically done on fabrics such as silk, cotton, and wool, and is characterized by its use of mirror-work, sequins, and beads. It is traditionally used to decorate clothing, household linens, and other textiles.

The folk arts of West India are an important part of the cultural heritage of the region and are known for their intricate designs, traditional themes, and the use of vibrant colors. These folk arts are an expression of the traditional way of life, customs, and beliefs of the people of West India. They are also an important source of income for many people in the region and help to promote the national identity of India.

ॐ

Writer Chitra Divakaruni emphasizes the importance of Indian folk arts and crafts, saying "traditional Indian art and craft forms are an ever-evolving river that meanders through each generation that has fed life into it". This quote signifies how folk arts and crafts have withstood the test of time, continuing to evolve and change, yet still retaining its essence. It is an ever-evolving form of art, embracing the positive changes incorporated by each generation yet maintaining its core.

IV

The Folk Arts of the South: An exploration of the traditional folk arts of South India

The Folk Arts of the South: An exploration of the traditional folk arts of South India, including Tanjore paintings, Kalamkari, and Pattachitra.

The folk arts of South India are a reflection of the rich cultural heritage of the region. They are an expression of the traditional way of life, customs, and beliefs of the people of South India. One of the most popular folk arts of South India is Tanjore painting. Tanjore paintings are traditional paintings that originated in the town of Thanjavur in Tamil

Nadu. They are known for their rich and vibrant colors, intricate details, and the use of gold leaf. The paintings typically depict Hindu gods and goddesses and are done on a wooden plank using a mixture of natural pigments, gold leaf, and gemstones.

Another traditional folk art of South India is Kalamkari. Kalamkari is a type of hand-painted or block-printed textile art that originated in Andhra Pradesh. The word "Kalamkari" means "pen craft" and refers to the use of a pen or a bamboo stick that is dipped in natural dyes to create the designs. Kalamkari textiles are known for their intricate and detailed designs, which depict scenes from Hindu mythology and epics such as the Ramayana and Mahabharata.

Pattachitra is another traditional folk art of South India, particularly in Odisha. Pattachitra is a type of painting that is done on a piece of cloth using natural dyes. The paintings depict scenes from Hindu mythology and are known for their vibrant colors and intricate details. Pattachitra paintings are typically done by Chitrakaras, a caste of painters who are specially trained in this art form.

The folk arts of South India are an important part of the cultural heritage of the region and are known for their rich and vibrant colors, intricate details, and traditional themes. These folk arts are an expression of the traditional way of life, customs, and beliefs of the people of South India. They are also an important source of income for many people in the region and help to promote the national identity of India.

ॐ

DR. JAGADEESH PILLAI

The stage artist Manul Jain suggests, "Great crafts often tell stories of India's long and varied history". Indian folk arts and crafts are a perfect example of this concept; they are more than just visual masterpieces, they are a reflection of the traditions, culture and beliefs of the community. They often tell stories of India's fascinating past that are preserved through generations.

৪৩

V

The Folk Arts of the East: An exploration of the traditional folk arts of East India

The Folk Arts of the East: An exploration of the traditional folk arts of East India, including Madhubani paintings, Dhokra metal casting, and Tussar silk.

The folk arts of East India are a reflection of the rich cultural heritage of the region. They are an expression of the traditional way of life, customs, and beliefs of the people of East India. One of the most popular folk arts of East India is Madhubani painting. Madhubani paintings are traditional paintings that originated in the Madhubani district of Bihar. They are known for their bright colors, bold geometric patterns, and the use of natural dyes. The paintings typically depict scenes from Hindu mythology, such as gods and goddesses and are done on a piece of paper or cloth using a mixture of natural pigments and a bamboo stick.

Another traditional folk art of East India is Dhokra metal casting. Dhokra metal casting is a traditional method of metal casting that originated in the state of Odisha. The method involves the use of the lost-wax casting technique to create intricate and detailed metal sculptures. Dhokra metal casting is known for its unique and complex designs, which are often inspired by nature and depict scenes from Hindu mythology.

Tussar silk is also a traditional folk art of East India, particularly in the states of West Bengal and Jharkhand. Tussar silk is a type of silk that is obtained from the larvae of certain species of silkworms. It is known for its natural golden color, soft texture, and durability. Tussar silk is used to make a variety of traditional textiles such as sarees, dupattas, and scarves.

The folk arts of East India are an important part of the cultural heritage of the region and are known for their bright colors, intricate designs, and traditional themes. These folk arts are an expression of the traditional way of life, customs, and beliefs of the people of East India. They are also an important source of income for many people in the region and help to promote the national identity of India.

ॐ

Author Salvatore Rubbino states " Indian art transports us back in time and shows us our roots". This holds true for all forms of Indian art, including folk art. Indian traditional art forms, such as warli art, rangoli, Kanthas, patachitra, and many others, are all representations of India's rich history and its people.

ॐ

VI

The Traditional Folk Arts of the Northeast

The Folk Arts of the Northeast: An exploration of the traditional folk arts of the Northeastern states of India, including the bamboo and cane crafts of Assam and Manipur, and the textile arts of Nagaland and Meghalaya.

The folk arts of the Northeastern states of India are a reflection of the rich cultural heritage of the region. They are an expression of the traditional way of life, customs, and beliefs of the people of the Northeastern states. One of the most popular folk arts of the Northeastern states is bamboo and cane craft. Bamboo and cane are widely available natural resources in the region, and are used to make a variety of handicrafts such as baskets, mats, and furniture. The bamboo and cane crafts of Assam and Manipur are known for their intricate designs and strong construction.

Another traditional folk art of the Northeastern states is the textile arts of Nagaland and Meghalaya. The textile arts of these states are known for their intricate designs, bold colors, and the use of natural dyes. The textiles are typically handwoven using locally sourced materials such as cotton, silk, and bamboo. The textiles are used to make a variety of traditional garments such as shawls, skirts, and headgears.

The folk arts of the Northeastern states are an important part of the cultural heritage of the region and are known for their intricate designs, bold colors, and traditional themes. These folk arts are an expression of the traditional way of life, customs, and beliefs of the people of the Northeastern states. They are also an important source of income for many people in the region and help to promote the national identity of India.

Poet Marjorie O'Bryan highlights the beauty of Indian folk art which says "The colors and textures of folk arts of India can make one feel alive and energized".

ಹ

VII

The Traditional Folk Music of India

The Folk Music of India: An exploration of the traditional folk music of India, including Bhavageethe, Baul, and Qawwali.

The folk music of India is a reflection of the rich cultural heritage of the country. It is an expression of the traditional way of life, customs, and beliefs of the people of India. One of the most popular folk music of India is Bhavageethe. Bhavageethe is a type of music that originated in the state of Karnataka, India. It is a form of poetry set to music and is known for its simple and melodious tunes. The lyrics of Bhavageethe are usually in the local language and reflect the everyday life and emotions of the people.

Another traditional folk music of India is Baul. Baul is a type of music that originated in the Bengal region of India and Bangladesh. It is known for its simple, yet powerful, lyrics and the use of traditional instruments such as the ektara (a one-stringed instrument), the dotara (a two-stringed instrument), and the khamak (a percussion instrument). Baul music is often accompanied by dancing and singing.

Qawwali is also a traditional folk music of India, particularly in the northern regions of the country. Qawwali is a type of devotional music that is associated with the Sufi tradition. It is known for its powerful and emotive lyrics and the use of a variety of traditional instruments such as the harmonium, tabla, and dholak. Qawwali music is usually performed in Muslim shrines, and it is believed to be a way to connect with the divine.

The folk music of India is an important part of the cultural heritage of the country. It is known for its simple and melodious tunes, traditional themes, and powerful lyrics. These folk music are an expression of the traditional way of life, customs, and beliefs of the people of India. They are also an important part of the Indian cultural heritage and help to preserve the traditional way of life and customs of the Indian people.

"Art is an expression of one's culture, and India's
traditional art forms embody its rich history and
creative spirit" (Avinash Pathak)

ॐ

VIII

The role of folk arts and crafts in Cultural Heritage of India

The Impact of Modernization on Indian Folk Arts and Crafts: An examination of the impact of modernization on Indian folk arts and crafts, and the efforts being made to preserve and promote them.

Modernization has had a significant impact on Indian folk arts and crafts. The rise of industrialization and globalization has led to a decrease in demand for traditional handicrafts and handloom products, as cheaper and mass-produced alternatives have become readily available. This has affected the livelihoods of artisans and craftspeople who depend on these traditional art forms for their income.

In addition to economic challenges, modernization has also led to a loss of traditional knowledge and skills. With the younger generation moving away from rural areas in search of better opportunities, the traditional knowledge and skills that have been passed down from generation to generation are at risk of being lost forever.

Despite these challenges, there are efforts being made to preserve and promote Indian folk arts and crafts. The government of India has implemented several schemes to provide financial assistance and support to artisans and promote their work. Non-government organizations (NGOs) and private organizations are also working to promote and preserve Indian folk arts and crafts by organizing exhibitions, workshops, and training programs.

Efforts are also being made to adapt traditional folk arts and crafts to modern tastes and trends. For example, traditional textile designs are being incorporated into contemporary fashion, and traditional wooden carvings are being used to decorate modern furniture. This helps to increase the demand for folk arts and crafts, and in turn, helps to preserve the traditional art forms.

Modernization has had a significant impact on Indian folk arts and crafts. However, efforts are being made to preserve and promote these traditional art forms. The government and private organizations are working to support the artisans and adapt traditional folk arts and crafts to modern tastes and trends. This helps to ensure that the traditional knowledge and skills are passed down to future generations and that these art forms remain an important part of the Indian cultural heritage.

"The Indian art and crafts represent the diversity and cultural sensibility of India's history" (Aditi Kapoor).

৪৩

IX

The Traditional Folk Dance of India

The Folk Dance of India: An exploration of the traditional folk dances of India, including Bhangra, Garba, and Bihu.

The folk dances of India are a reflection of the rich cultural heritage of the country. They are an expression of the traditional way of life, customs, and beliefs of the people of India. One of the most popular folk dances of India is Bhangra. Bhangra is a type of dance that originated in the Punjab region of India and Pakistan. It is known for its high energy and fast-paced beats, and is traditionally performed by men. Bhangra is usually performed during the harvest festival of Vaisakhi.

Another traditional folk dance of India is Garba. Garba is a type of dance that originated in Gujarat, India. It is known for its complex footwork and the use of traditional instruments such as the dhol and the garba. Garba is traditionally performed by women and is usually accompanied by singing and the playing of traditional instruments. It is performed during the festival of Navaratri.

Bihu is another traditional folk dance of India, particularly in the state of Assam. Bihu is a type of dance that is associated with the Bihu festival, which marks the beginning of the Assamese New Year. The dance is known for its energetic moves and the use of traditional instruments such as the dhol, pepa (a type of flute) and taal (a type of cymbals). Bihu is usually performed by both men and women, and it is accompanied by singing and the playing of traditional instruments.

The folk dances of India are an important part of the cultural heritage of the country. They are known for their high energy, traditional themes, and the use of traditional instruments. These folk dances are an expression of the traditional way of life, customs, and beliefs of the people of India. They are also an important part of the Indian cultural heritage and help to preserve the traditional way

continue

of life and customs of the Indian people. These dances are usually performed during festivals and other special occasions, and they bring together communities and families to celebrate and honor their cultural heritage.

Folk dances in India also have many different styles and forms, each with their own unique characteristics and history. For example, the Kathak dance from North India, is known for its intricate footwork and storytelling aspect, whereas the Kuchipudi dance from Andhra Pradesh, is known for its expressive gestures and dramatic performances.

The folk dances of India are also an important aspect of the Indian tourism industry. They attract many tourists from all over the world who come to India to explore the country's rich cultural heritage. The folk dances of India are also an important source of revenue for the government and help to promote the national economy.

In conclusion, the folk dances of India are an integral part of the Indian cultural heritage. They are a reflection of the traditional way of life, customs, and beliefs of the people of India. They are a medium through which the traditional knowledge, skills, and creativity of the Indian people are passed down from generation to generation. They are an important source of livelihood for many people in rural India, a symbol of the rich cultural diversity of the country, and an important aspect of the Indian tourism industry.

"The skill, finesse and passion that goes into making
Indian crafts is a special kind of art" (Chetna Goklani).

X

The Traditional Folk Festivals of India

The Folk Festivals of India: An exploration of the traditional folk festivals of India, including Holi, Diwali, and Pongal.

The folk festivals of India are a reflection of the rich cultural heritage of the country. They are an expression of the traditional way of life, customs, and beliefs of the people of India. One of the most popular folk festivals of India is Holi. Holi is a festival of colors that is celebrated in the month of March. It marks the arrival of spring and the victory of good over evil. During the festival, people play with colored powder and water, and visit friends and family to exchange sweets and greetings.

Another traditional folk festival of India is Diwali. Diwali is a festival of lights that is celebrated in the month of October or November. It marks the victory of good over evil and the triumph of light over darkness. During the festival, people light diyas (clay lamps) and candles, and decorate their homes with rangolis (colorful floor designs). It is also a festival of sweets, firework, and shopping.

Pongal is another traditional folk festival of India, particularly in the southern states of Tamil Nadu, Andhra Pradesh, and KarnATAKA. Pongal is a harvest festival that is celebrated in the month of January. It marks the end of the winter solstice and the beginning of the harvest season. During the festival, people prepare Pongal, a sweet dish made of rice, milk, and jaggery, and offer it to the Sun God. They also decorate their homes with kolams (rice flour patterns), and engage in bull taming sports.

The folk festivals of India are an important part of the cultural heritage of the country. They are known for their vibrant colors, traditional themes, and the celebration of nature, culture and religion. These festivals are an expression of the traditional way of life, customs, and beliefs of the people of India. They are also an important part of the Indian cultural heritage and help to preserve the traditional way of life and customs of the Indian people. It brings together communities and families to celebrate and honor their cultural heritage.

"It's not just any art that needs to be painted to become beautiful. Some forms of art, like India's traditional art, become so because of its soul" (Shilpa Ramesh)

XI

The Impact of Modernization on Indian Folk Arts and Crafts

The Impact of Modernization on Indian Folk Arts and Crafts: An examination of the impact of modernization on Indian folk arts and crafts, and the efforts being made to preserve and promote them.

Modernization has had a significant impact on Indian folk arts and crafts. With the introduction of new technology, mass production methods, and global trade, traditional folk arts and crafts have been facing competition from mass-produced goods. This has led to a decline in the demand for folk arts and crafts, and in turn, has affected the livelihoods of the artisans who depend on these traditional art forms for their livelihood.

One of the major impacts of modernization on Indian folk arts and crafts has been the loss of traditional knowledge and skills. With the younger generation moving away from rural areas in search of better opportunities, the traditional knowledge and skills that have been passed down from generation to generation are at risk of being lost forever.

Despite these challenges, there are efforts being made to preserve and promote Indian folk arts and crafts. The government of India has implemented several schemes to provide financial assistance and support to artisans and promote their work. Non-government organizations (NGO's) and private organizations are also working to promote and preserve Indian folk arts and crafts by organizing exhibitions, workshops, and training programs.

Efforts are also being made to adapt traditional folk arts and crafts to modern tastes and trends. For example, traditional textile designs are being incorporated into contemporary fashion, and traditional wooden carvings are being used to decorate modern furniture. This helps to increase the demand for folk arts and crafts, and in turn, helps to preserve the traditional art forms.

Modernization has had a significant impact on Indian folk arts and crafts. However, efforts are being made to preserve and promote these traditional art forms. The government and private organizations are working to support the artisans and adapt traditional folk arts and crafts to modern tastes and trends. This helps to ensure that the traditional knowledge and skills are passed down to future generations and that these art forms remain an important part of the Indian cultural heritage.

Other Books Of The Author

1. The Moments When I Met God
2. Kashiyile Theertha Pathangal
3. GURU GYAN VANI
4. Abhiprerak Gita
5. ASSI SE JAIN GHAT TAK
6. Hopelessness of Arjuna
7. The Soul and It's True Nature
8. Sense of Action (Karma)
9. Action through Wisdom
10. Action through Wisdom
11. THEORY AND PRACTICAL OF EVERY ACTION
12. LOGICAL UNDERSTANDING OF THE SUPREME
13. THE IMPERISHABLE SUPREME
14. Yatra Nishadraj se Hanuman Ghat Tak
15. Yatra Karnatak Ghat se Raja Ghat Tak
16. Yatra Pandey Ghat se Prayagraj Ghat Tak
17. Yatra Ranjendra Prasad Ghat se Dattatreya Ghat Tak
18. YaatraSindhiya Ghat se Gwaliar Ghat Tak
19. Yatra Mangala Gauri Ghat se Hanuman Gadhi Ghat Tak
20. Yatra Gaay Ghat Se Nishad Ghat Tak
21. MAA GANGA, GHATEN EVM UTSAV
22. Ganga Arti Dev Deepavali evam Any Utsav
23. Potentials of Digitalized India
24. VEDIC CONSCIOUSNESS
25. A Brief Introduction to Vedic Science
26. Kashi ke Barah Jyotirling
27. IMPACT OF MOTIVATION
28. Let's have a Milky Way Journey
29. Color Therapy in a Nutshell

59. The Holistic Cow: A Look at the Physical, Spiritual, and Cultural Importance of Cows in India
60. Arts of Healing
61. Exploring the Divine
62. Understanding Five Elements
63. The Etymology of Ram
64. Symbols of India
65. Voice of Change (About Speeches of Great Men)
66. She Speaks (About Speeches of Great Women)
67. **Patriotism on Celluloid – Brief About Patriotic Films**
68. **The Music of Motivation: A Brief Guide to Inspirational Film Songs**
69. **Unlocking the Secrets of the Dashopanishads**
70. A Cultural Mosaic
71. Ancient Traditions, Modern Minds
72. Ecos of Ancient Wisdom
73. Beneath the Surface
74. From Temples to Ashrams
75. Sages of the Subcontinent
76. The Art of Healling (Ayurveda, Yoga & Naturopathy)
77. Indian Kitchen
78. The Festivals of India
79. The Indian Epics Retold
80. The Power of Mantras
81. The Indian River Ganges
82. The Indian Architecture
83. Rites of Passage
84. The Indian Silk Road
85. The Indian Literature
86. The Indian Villages
87. The Indian Folks & Crafts

୫

Contact

DR. JAGADEESH PILLAI

PhD in Vedic Science

Four Times Guinness World Record Holder

Winner of Mahatma Gandhi Vishwa Shanti Puraskar and
Global Peace Ambassador

Gemology, Astro & Vastu Consultant - Spiritual Counselor

Consultant for designing World Record Ideas

Efficient Tarot Card Reader

9839093003

myrichindia@gmail.com

drjagadeeshpillai@facebook

drjagadeeshpillai@instagram

jagadeeshpillai@youtube

www. JAGADEESHPILLAI.com

|| LOKAHA SAMASTHAHA SUKHINO BHAVANTU ||